To parents and teachers

We hope you and the children will enjoy reading this story in either English or French. The story is simple, but not *simplified*, so the language of the French and the English is quite natural but there is lots of repetition.

At the back of the book is a small picture dictionary with the key words and how to pronounce them. There is also a simple pronunciation guide to the whole story on the last page.

Here are a few suggestions on using the book:

- Read the story aloud in English first, to get to know it. Treat it like any other picture book: look at the pictures, talk about the story and the characters and so on.

- Then look at the picture dictionary and say the French names for the key words. Ask the children to repeat them. Concentrate on speaking the words out loud, rather than reading them.

- Go back and read the story again, this time in English *and* French. Don't worry if your pronunciation isn't quite correct. Just have fun trying it out. Check the guide at the back of the book, if necessary, but you'll soon pick up how to say the French words.

- When you think you and the children are ready, you can try reading the story in French only. Ask the children to say it with you. Only ask them to read it if they are eager to try. The spelling could be confusing and put them off.

- Above all encourage the children to have a go and give lots of praise. Little children are usually quite unselfconscious and this is excellent for building up confidence in a foreign language.

First edition for the United States and Canada published 1994 by Barron's Educational Series, Inc.
Text © Copyright 1994 by b small publishing, Surrey, England
Illustrations © Copyright 1994 by Steve Weatherill
All rights reserved. No part of this book may be reproduced in any form, by photostat, microfilm, xerography, or any other means, or incorporated into any information retrieval system, electronic or mechanical, without the written permission of the copyright owner.
Address all inquiries to: Barron's Educational Series, Inc., 250 Wireless Boulevard, Hauppauge, New York 11788
ISBN-13: 978-0-8120-6454-4   Library of Congress Catalog Card Number 94-561
ISBN-10: 0-8120-6454-2   19 18 17 16 15 14 13 12
Printed in Shenzhen Wing King Tong Paper Product Co. Ltd. Shenzhen Guangdong China
Date of Manufacture: January 2011

I'm too big

Je suis trop gros

Lone Morton

From an idea by Ella McCourt

Pictures by Steve Weatherill
French by Ide Marie Hélie

BARRON'S

I'm too big.

Je suis trop gros.

I'm too tall.

Je suis trop grande.

I want a long neck.

Je veux un long cou.

I want big ears.

Je veux de grandes oreilles.

I don't like my long nose!
I want a short one.

Je n'aime pas mon long nez!
J'en veux un court.

I don't like my long neck!
I want a short one.

Je n'aime pas mon long cou.
J'en veux un court.

I don't like grey.
I want to be yellow like you

Je n'aime pas le gris.
Je veux être jaune comme toi.

I like grey.
I want to be grey like you.

J'aime le gris.
Je veux être grise comme toi.

But I want shorter legs …

Mais je veux des pattes plus courtes …

... and a bigger head.

... et une tête plus grosse.

I want a longer tail ...

Je veux une queue plus longue ...

… and a smaller head.

… et une tête plus petite.

Yes, I want a longer tail ...

Oui, je veux une queue plus longue ...

… and a longer nose.

… et un nez plus long.

But wait!
I like you as you are.

Mais attends!
Je t'aime comme tu es.

And you're fine as you are.

Toi aussi, tu es bien comme tu es.

Yes ... we're great like this!

Oui ... nous sommes très bien comme ça!

Pronouncing French

Don't worry if your pronunciation isn't quite correct. The important thing is to be willing to try.

  The pronunciation guide here will help but it cannot be completely accurate:

- Read the guide as naturally as possible, as if it were English.
- Put stress on the letters in *italics,* e.g., lombool-*onss.*
- Don't roll the r at the end of the word, for example in the French word **le** (the): ler.

If you can, ask a French person to help and move on as soon as possible to speaking the words without the guide.

Note: French adjectives usually have two forms, one for masculine and one for feminine nouns. They often look very similar but are pronounced slightly differently, e.g., **petit** and **petite** (see on the right).

Words Les Mots

leh moh

grey

gris/grise

gree/greez

yellow

jaune

shown

big

gros/grosse
gro/gross

grand/grande
grohn/grond

tall

grand/grande
grohn/grond

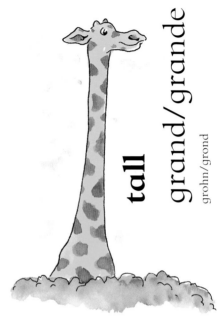

small

petit/petite
p'tee/p'teet

short

court/courte
koor/koort

long

long/longue
loh/longer

head

la tête

lah tet

nose

le nez

ler neh

tail

la queue

lah ker

leg

la patte

lah pat

ear

l'oreille

lor-*ay*

neck

le cou

ler coo

A simple guide to pronouncing this French story

Je suis trop gros.
sh' swee troh gro

Je suis trop grande.
sh' swee troh grond

Je veux un long cou.
sh' verz ahn loh coo

Je veux de grandes oreilles.
sh' ver der gronds or-*ay*

Je n'aime pas mon long nez!
sh' nem pah moh loh neh

J'en veux un court.
shon verz ahn koor

Je n'aime pas mon long cou!
sh' nem pah moh loh coo

J'en veux un court.
shon verz ahn koor

Je n'aime pas le gris.
sh' nem pah ler gree

Je veux être jaune comme toi.
sh' verz et-r' shown com twah

J'aime le gris.
shem ler gree

Je veux être grise comme toi.
sh' verz et-r' greez com twah

Mais je veux des pattes plus courtes ...
meh sh' ver deh pat ploo koort

et une tête plus grosse.
eh yoon tet ploo gross

Je veux une queue plus longue ...
sh' verz yoon ker ploo *longer*

et une tête plus petite.
eh yoon tet ploo p'teet

Oui, je veux une queue plus longue ...
wee sh' verz yoon ker ploo *longer*

et un nez plus long.
eh ahn neh ploo loh

Mais attends!
meh at-*toh*!

Je t'aime comme tu es.
sh' tem com too eh

Toi aussi, tu es bien comme tu es.
twah oh-see, too eh bee-*yahn* com too eh

Oui ... nous sommes très bien comme ça!
wee ... noo som treh bee-*yahn* com sah!